HAPPY

Finding Happiness In A Crazy Ass World

MARK LLEWHELLIN

DEDICATION

This book is dedicated to the love of my life, my little miracle, Léon James Llewhellin, who I love more than anyone in the world. You are kind, thoughtful, well balanced and you are already achieving great things in your life!

Words cannot describe how much I love you and how proud I am of the person you are.

This book is also dedicated to you the reader. May you also live a happy life.

GET TWO OF MARK'S BOOKS FOR FREE

Join Mark's team for information on new books along with special offers and pick up a FREE copy of Mark's 5 star reviewed books:

'The Underdog' and 'Delusions Of Grandeur.'

Details can be found at the end of this book.

TABLE OF CONTENTS

INTRODUCTION

"When I was five years old, my mother always told me that happiness was the key to life. When I went to school, they asked me what I wanted to be when I grew up. I wrote down happy. They told me I didn't understand the assignment, and I told them they didn't understand life."
John Lennon

Happy

.

With this book I decided to home in on a subject that is one of the most important to most human beings; the subject of happiness.

I think you'll agree, there's nothing in this world that is more important to your life and the lives of the people you love than happiness.

Happiness is right up there with health in terms of what is most important in our lives!

So, if happiness is one of the most important things to master during our lifetime, then why isn't it on the national curriculum?

I doubt very much if you've ever been taught anything on the subject?

Throughout your whole time in school you probably didn't even do one lesson on it!

Zero, nothing, nada, zip, zilch, not one jot, diddlysquat, jack shit... sweet FA!

One of the things that most people want in life is happiness, but very few people learn about happiness and how to be happier.

Why?

It's like society has a belief that you are either happy or you're not and that's the end of the story.

However, I believe that if you want to excel at something then you're going to have to learn about that very subject.

From my own perspective, if you have a natural talent for a particular thing you can always improve by learning more about it.

Sometimes you'll see people who always seem to be happy both publicly and behind closed doors.

They walk down the street with a smile on their face and look as if they don't have a care in the world!

Happier people have more doors open for them, they're luckier people, they walk around with a spring in their step and a glint in their eyes.

Other happy people walk around with a quiet, calm confidence and when the shit hits the fan in life, many of those people have the ability to handle it better mentally!

Happier people also don't get ill as much and when they do get ill they usually recover quicker and have more energy and vitality in life!

So here's a question, are you happy at least 95 – 99% of the time?

If you are, that's fantastic!

If you're not, then you're selling yourself short.

You're not only selling yourself short on a daily, weekly, or monthly basis, you are also selling yourself short with your entire life!

I'm a happy person most of the time, so I decided to do a self-analysis and delve into why I'm happy most of the time, and then write it down and help others, so this is how the book you're now reading came to be.

Throughout this self-analysis, I kept asking myself the question, "Could I be even happier and if so, how?"

Of course there are obviously times in life when I'm not

happy.

I'm still a human being and I still have emotions like most other people, so I can still be emotionally hurt and experience sad and unhappy times.

When I've lost family that are very close to me, it wasn't as if I was in the hospital next to the deathbed opening a bottle of bubbly and celebrating.

Although, I might have been if I was left with a very large inheritance... I'm joking!

If you have people that you love dearly and have lost, you know exactly what I'm talking about.

For over 25 years I have done research on psychology, philosophy, and personal development so I could become happier and more successful in different areas of my life, and I'm still learning new things.

Doing this has made a massive positive difference in my life and I've achieved some pretty cool things, but even more importantly than any of my achievements, I've been lucky enough to be happy most of the time too!

Can you train your mind so that you can be happy 100% of the time?

From what I've learned about people, it's possible to be happy most of the time, but to be happy 100% of the time is highly unlikely, and if there is an individual on this planet that has been happy 100% of the time, I have never come across them.

In order to be happy 100% of the time you would have to:

1. Never have been hurt mentally.

2. Never have experienced any physical pain.

Without wanting to sound pessimistic or negative, the chances of anyone not experiencing these two things as they go through life is zero!

That's just reality, and it's part of the deal we're all given while we're here on Earth.

Let's face it, there'll be some challenges that you'll go through in life that will be as welcome as a turd in a swimming pool!

There will be times when you'll get totally blindsided by life!

One minute, your life is going great, and the next minute, everything turns into one epic shit show!

This can be anything from losing the job that you thought was secure, losing a relationship that you thought was going well, or it could be the loss of a loved one just to name a few things.

Whatever you go through in life, the most important thing is to get back on track and find happiness in your life!

Like you, I certainly prefer to be happy more often than not.

Also, I realise we all have different lives, and I am only one person, so I have limited experiences and there is still much that I have to learn in life.

To that end, I not only use my own life experiences in this book, but I also draw off the experiences of other people and have done extensive research on the subject of happiness to provide you with the best information that I can.

In this book, my goal is to help you get out of your negative mindset when you feel down, and to help you shift over to a more positive mindset that will lead to a happier and healthier life.

We're all unique so there's not one set of rules for all, just like there's not one set of rules for every person losing weight.

Running and eating heathy is one of the best ways to lose weight.

However, if you have arthritis in your knees, or if you have no legs, you'll have to find a different form of exercise (although eating healthy will always work), you'll have to find what works for you and it's the same with happiness.

In other words, simply take out of this book what works for you.

There is no one definitive guide to happiness; there is only a guide because we are all different!

Not only that, the world is constantly changing, and as we move forward we will all have unique experiences in life.

Also, just because this is a book on happiness with the lovely smiling emoji on the front cover, it doesn't mean that we're not going to get down into the nitty-gritty of things that need to be addressed.

It's not as if nothing bad will ever happen in your life.

We all know that's not the reality.

In other words, your life has either:

"Just come out of a shit storm, you're currently in a shit storm, or you're heading into a shit storm!"

It wouldn't be right if I simply fluffed over the challenges that we'll all face with happy, happy, happy words in this book, without addressing the realities of life.

There is only so much I can put in this book about finding more happiness; however, you'll find more information on the subject of happiness throughout certain chapters of almost all of my personal development books because of the importance it has in our lives.

My goal with this book is to make a positive difference to your life.

I'm hoping that you'll discover a few things in this book that will add to the overall quality of your life and make you a happier person; I feel that if you take one positive thing from this book and it makes you happier, then this book has served its purpose and writing it will have been worthwhile.

"The most important thing is to enjoy your life,
to be happy."
Audrey Hepburn

1 – HAPPY GENES

"Make the best use of what is in your power and take the rest as it happens."

Epictetus

Happy

Ok so let's start at the beginning of what can affect happiness.

One thing that we have to factor into our happiness is: how much of our happiness is to do with our genetics?

Is it God given or luck?

And if genes do play a role in our happiness, how much so?

The website PositivePsychology.com reported that a meta-analysis study conducted at Stanford University showed the role that genetics play in depression.

It concluded that an absence of depression is not an indicator of the presence of happiness.

They also studied the 5-HTTLPR gene which showed that the more people that have this certain type of gene (which is a serotonin transporter gene), the higher the levels of satisfaction and happiness they have.

Another study from the Minnesota Twin Registry reported that 50% of life satisfaction boils down to genetics.

Many other studies report that 40 to 50% of our lives and subsequent happiness stems from our genetics.

I did consider writing a longer chapter on genetics, however there was simply no point because at the end of the day, what we've been given, is what we've been given, and we have to make the very best of it!

Moreover, many people will try to use this as a crutch.

In other words, if genetics are responsible for 40 – 50% of our happiness, many people may feel as if their happiness is out of their control. This could push their unhappiness up to levels of 95% or even 100% because they will use it as an excuse.

And if you're like me or 99.9% of the population, the chances are you've never even been tested for this gene, so you won't even know.

So to what amount do the things that happen to us in life contribute towards our happiness?

This is ultimately down to the individual as we're all different, and different situations affect us all in their own unique ways.

The exciting thing is that you can grow stronger mentally through learning and understanding how your thoughts work.

If I can become excessively strong mentally and happy (most of the time), then so can you!

However, if you want to succeed at most things in life, you'll have to put the time and effort in. I have spent over 25 years putting time and effort into learning about psychology, happiness, and personal development!

I humbled myself by learning from the people that have gone before me and it's changed my life in the most amazing ways!

When you feed your mind with this type of information, you're not going to turn into some terminator type machine, or any other kind of robot, in which you have no emotions.

There will be times when you will still get really hurt and are unhappy.

However, with time and patience, you can learn to become a phenomenally strong person mentally and get back to happiness quicker than ever before!

For most of us, our starting point as a baby was shortly after we were born.

What is one of the first things that babies do when they are born?

There aren't many babies that are born with a big smile on their face and full of the joys of the world!

Nope, most of us are bawling our eyes out and are extremely upset!

So, if we're not crying in distress like we were on the day we were born, then there is only one way to go... And that way is up!

2 – THE "I'LL BE HAPPY WHEN" STORY

"Plenty of people miss their share of happiness, not because they never found it, but because they didn't stop to enjoy it."
William Feather

Happy

You may have fallen into the trap that millions of people, if not billions of people throughout history have fallen into.

They have fallen into a trap of believing that they'll be happy when they reach a certain goal.

However, the reality to this way of thinking can unfortunately lead to a lot of misery along the journey because you're more focused on the current situation you're in and not where you want to be!

Have you ever told yourself, "I'll be happy when... (fill in the blank)"

I know I have.

The ironic thing about that type of thinking is, when you reach your goal, it's usually satisfying for a brief moment, and then you decide to set your next goal, and think to yourself, I'll be happy when I achieve this next goal!

Before you know it, you're like a little puppy dog chasing its tail, trying to catch something that you'll seldom catch.

Even if you do catch it, and experience that brief moment of happiness, many people let go of that happiness because they're after their next goal and won't be happy until they reach that goal.

Does this sound familiar?

The 'I'll be happy when' story we make up in our own minds is a classic bullshit story that we often tell ourselves, which by its very existence cuts out 99% of the happiness throughout our entire lives.

Crazy isn't it?

Sadly, many of these people aren't even aware what they're doing, which shouldn't be the case for us after we've read and digested these words.

I have a coffee mug that says:

"Happiness is not a destination, it's a way of life."

When the COVID-19 pandemic hit in 2020, many

countries around the world got shut down to one extent or another and many people had to stop going to work.

Some people loved it, and some people hated it.

For some of the ones that still had accommodation and could still afford to eat, many of them decided to embrace the change and the slow pace of life if they were furloughed and therefore off work.

Many of these people decided to enjoy not having to get up in the morning and be at work at a certain time.

They decided to enjoy their families more, they decided to enjoy their free time more, and they decided to enjoy nature and life a lot more too!

It was as if they had suddenly come out of the rat race and didn't give a shit about who had what! They simply enjoyed what they had in life.

In other words:

"If you're too busy to stop and appreciate everything that you have and everything that you've achieved, you will never be happy, and you will have failed in one of the most important areas in life!"

I've written a book called 'Grab Life By The Balls' (which hasn't been released at the time of this book getting published) which talks about living life to the full; it also incorporates surveys about what people want most in life and their regrets.

I won't go into the specific details in this book as I've covered it in 'Grab Life By The Balls' but this point is still worth mentioning:

One of the top regrets people had when coming to the end of their lives was that they felt they had worked too much!

This next quote sums it up nicely:

"When all is said and done, success without happiness is the worst kind of failure." – Louis Binstock

Just before I started writing this part about enjoying the journey and being happy in the present I was playing on my son's wrestling game.

I know... here I am, an ex Army Commando and bodyguard and I'm playing on games that were mainly designed for children to play.

I even remember listening to some of my friends talking about playing these types of games and thought, "you're in your 20's, 30's and 40's, I can't believe you're playing these games at your age," funny how things turn around sometimes.

At one time, I did get a little bit hooked on playing a superhero game called 'Injustice' on my iPad.

Sometimes we get hooked on these things, and we do certain activities as a way of avoiding something that we should be doing to move us forward in the game of life. This was something I ended up doing and this is something we need to be aware of.

I was telling myself that playing this game was vital because I could win Léon some more characters for his games, which was really a load of crap!

I did feel a sense of escapism in which I got the feeling of going back to being more like a child, not having to be concerned about the stresses of adult life, where you're in a world governed and judged to a large extent by status, money, achievement, taxes, and control.

However, there also comes a point where we have to deal with these things, take our head out of the sand and face life's challenges head on.

As I've said just before writing this piece, I noticed that I was playing on Léon's wrestling game just for the sake of building credits and getting a new character for him (or so I told myself!).

I actually got to the point of not enjoying what I was doing; I was more focused on getting the prize than enjoying the game and this is what we often do in life.

We are so obsessed with the end result that we stop living in the present and enjoying the now.

We all dream about possibilities for the future whether it's that new car, the new house, the dream holiday, or the latest gadget that we want, but it's important to enjoy the journey because that's what life is made of!

On the subject of Léon and his games, he was playing a game called 'Subway Surfer' and after every game he said to me, "have we got enough coins to buy someone new Daddy?"

Like many other games you win coins by doing well in the games.

At first I didn't mind him saying this, we all want to make progress of some sort in our lives, but this got to the stage where he was asking if we had enough coins after every single game.

After the fourth or fifth game I had had enough of this question because he was focusing too much on the next new thing and not enjoying the character he was playing with.

I asked him not to keep asking me this question (as he was about 100 games off winning a new character) and to simply enjoy playing the game.

Yes it's good to get the reward at the end of the game, but he needed to enjoy the journey as well.

So it wasn't just an adult challenge, it's also something children go through too.

If you've got to a stage of focusing on the next thing all the time and no longer enjoying the moment, then stop and think about how much time you're wasting.

You're literally wishing your whole life away!

So remember, it's great to have something to look forward to, but enjoy the moment as well.

Also, if you take the right steps and enjoy the moment, while you're putting the effort into achieving your next goal, the chances are you will have achieved that next goal before you know it, as time will have flown by!

One of the things I love about running or cycling, when you're not in a race, is that the journey can be a lot more important than the destination.

The destination can be great, and you can be happy that you've got to your destination, but most of the time you'll be working towards your next goal, so it would make sense to find things to be happy about right now, rather than just being happy at one point in time when you've achieved that goal.

In summary:

Don't become a bore and take life too seriously, stop to enjoy the little things!

"Learn to enjoy every minute of your life. Be happy now. Don't wait for something outside yourself to make you happy in the future. Think how really precious the time is you have to spend, whether it's at work or with your family. Every minute should be enjoyed and savoured."
Earl Nightingale

3 – THINK POSITIVE THOUGHTS BEFORE YOU GO TO SLEEP

"Very little is needed to make a happy life, it is all within yourself, in your way of thinking."
Marcus Aurelius

Happy

The scientific study of dreams is called oneirology. Dreams mainly occur during the 'rapid eye movement' (REM) stage of sleep, when our brain activity is high, which resembles the state of being awake. Just in case you were wondering, yes, the band, R.E.M. was named after this dream state condition.

According to research, we have between 3 to 7 dreams a night.

Even though we have many dreams while we're asleep, it's the dreams that happen just before we wake up that are the dreams that we remember.

Have you ever had a dream, and you woke up straight after that dream and was able to remember that dream?

One morning, I had just woken up after a dream.

Unfortunately, this dream was far from pleasant; it was

more of a nightmare than a nice pleasant dream.

In this dream, for some reason the police were after me because of something to do with computer hacking a big business.

All I remember was that I was being treated like this major computer hacker who had done something, and they were waiting for their opportunity to arrest me.

I remember thinking in the dream, do I go on the run and try to avoid them, or do I just hand myself in?

The dream led to a scenario in which I was on my way to an appointment, which I knew they would've known about.

I also knew this was the best opportunity they had to arrest me.

It wasn't long after that I woke up.

As I woke up, I could remember feeling upset, disappointed, and as though I had failed in life.

The interesting thing about this was it felt real, I mean really real!

Of course in my real world none of this was true (especially the part about being clever enough to be a high-level computer hacker), but regardless of it not being true, I truly believed it was until I woke up and came back to reality!

How many times do we think about something, or worry about something that isn't even real?

I know I've done it many times in the past, and when you think about it, it's a little bit crazy because that situation isn't happening, but you think that it might, and you start to feel bad about it or upset about it.

You're visualising something going wrong, and of course that never makes you feel good, which in turn makes you feel unhappy.

A lot of this has to do with an inbuilt system that we have, which is passed down from our early ancestors and is just trying to protect us.

So, trying to override that basic human system isn't the easiest of things to do, but we can do it if we focus and concentrate enough on positive thoughts.

When a negative thought comes into your mind, it is important that you immediately replace it with a positive one.

This takes self-awareness and a conscious effort to put this into practice.

All too often we go into autopilot, which makes us feel bad, and if we stay on autopilot and don't consciously take charge of the controls of our mind, we'll keep feeling bad on a regular basis, which can ruin our lives!

For me, to wake up feeling unhappy and scared about a situation was extremely rare, and it made me think why this had happened.

Why did I wake up frightened I thought to myself?

I traced it back to the evening before where I had been watching the TV and had come across several negative stories, which were very tragic.

Because those stories were one of the last things on my mind that evening, I went to bed with negative thoughts.

However, those negative thoughts didn't end as soon as I went to sleep, there was a very good chance that I dreamt about them more than once in the night, and of course, when I woke up in the morning, I was still stuck in a negative mindset.

One of the stories was about the spread of the COVID-19 virus.

It talked about how many people it had killed and the mess that the economy was in as a direct result of the pandemic.

Another story was about American basketball superstar Kobe Bryant and his daughter getting killed in a helicopter crash.

Before I woke up from the dream about the police being after me and realising that I was looking at a long prison sentence, I also remember having a dream about the helicopter crash.

It wasn't a clear dream, but I can remember the dream feeling very real, and it was as if I was in the helicopter looking on as a spectator.

So, what's the moral of the story?

Focus on positive thoughts before you sleep.

When you wake up in the morning, you are likely to wake up with the thoughts you had just before you went to sleep.

For example, three positive thoughts I often have before I go to sleep (at the time of writing) are.

1. How grateful I am to have such an amazing son.

2. I am so grateful to live the lucky life I live.

3. I also tell myself that I'm a successful and highly prolific author, because it is one of my main goals at the time of writing these words.

Let's look at some negative things I've thought about in the past.

Maybe you've thought similar things:

1. I can't believe that person did that to me!

2. What a mess my life is in!

3. What if I lose (fill in the blank)!

It doesn't take a brain surgeon to work out what set of thoughts would make me happier and sleep better.

You can write down or think about your own three things that you can use before you go to sleep at night:

1. I'm so grateful for…

2. I'm grateful to live…

3. I am a successful…

There are certain things that I don't always say to myself such as:

- I am a great Dad.

Or

- I am a good runner.

The reason for this is because those things are already part of who I am, so my subconscious mind already believes it.

In other words, there is no need to convince myself that I need to become it, because I live it.

You'll find that it's the same with you.

There are certain things that you know that you're good at, and you don't have to spend any conscious time trying to convince yourself that you are good at it.

You just are!

What you say to your loved ones before you go to sleep will also make a big difference.

What do you think I say to my son before he goes to sleep?

I always say words to Léon such as:

- My champion.

- World's best Son.

And

- Love you Léon.

When I do this, he goes to sleep knowing that the person closest to him (along with his Mum) believes in him and loves him.

So, just to summarise, when you're sleeping, your subconscious mind is working away, and your subconscious mind will work either for you or against you!

4 – GET ENOUGH SLEEP

"Sleep is the best meditation."
Dalai Lama

Happy

The two important questions here are:

1. How important is it to get the right amount of sleep?

2. How much sleep do we need?

The answer to question one is extremely important!

The second question isn't quite as easy to answer, as there are many different factors that will determine how much sleep you need, age being one of the main ones.

Obviously, babies and children need a lot more sleep because they are in a rapid growing phase.

I was listening to Arnold Schwarzenegger one day on the Tim Ferris Podcast, and he said something very much in line with my own thoughts on how much sleep we need.

Arnie said when he was in his late teens he would need

around 9 hours sleep, but now in his later years, he usually sleeps for 6 hours and that's enough for him.

At the age of 46 (at the time of writing) I also sleep for around 6 hours and find that's enough for me, but it can also go up to seven or eight hours depending on how badly I need it.

However, the age and the time we should sleep for isn't the same for everyone.

There are no exact rules to follow for how much sleep you should get as everybody is different.

What is very important is to get enough sleep so that you feel refreshed in the morning, and you can go out and have a really productive day!

I remember when I was in the Army (and maybe still now for some people) you would hear things like, "you can sleep when you're dead," which was basically making reference to getting by on less sleep, so you could spend that time working on a goal.

If that is what you want to do then that's fine, as long as you don't go through your day saying things like, "I'm so tired, I've been up since 5am, 4am, 2am" or whatever else it is.

Some people like to try and impress others by saying how early they get up, how late they go to bed and how busy they are, which is something I personally get bored of hearing.

"Oh so you haven't had much sleep, would you like a medal for that?"

"Oh so you're really busy? Join the hundreds millions of other people all over the world that are also busy."

When it comes to some of the highest achievers in the world of health and fitness, such as Olympic athletes or sports stars, you will hear some of them talk about how important getting the right amount of sleep is for their training.

When it comes to finances, the richest man in the world, at the time of writing, Jeff Bezos, is reported to sleep a good eight hours a day!

Just to put a final nail in the coffin that sleeping for only four or five hours a day will make you more of an achiever in life; Albert Einstein was reported to sleep for around 10 hours a day!

One of my major goals in life was to have a lifestyle in which I could sleep as much as I wanted to and get up whenever I wanted.

Although I'm lucky enough to live that life now, I still remember what it was like to wake up to an alarm for at least five days a week.

I can't say that it was something I enjoyed; however, it was necessary at the time to get by until I reached my goal of getting up when I wanted to.

If you're dragging yourself out of bed in the morning then you probably need more sleep, so you'll have to make a conscious effort to go to bed earlier.

I know it's not rocket science is it?

However, when we have a goal to hit, or there is some sort of deadline hanging over us, sometimes we have to put in the late hours and get the job done.

The question we have to ask ourselves is, "how important is it to reach my target in relation to the quality of my life and my mental health?"

If you are staying up late some nights to hit goals, and you don't manage to get your full sleep in, it's not the end of the world.

However, if you're doing this night in, night out for months on end, then it'll have a negative effect on both your mental health and your body.

When I don't get enough sleep, I start to get agitated at minor distractions, which hinders my creative thinking and process for writing and production.

Think about how you function when you haven't had enough sleep.

One of the masters of ancient Greek literature 'Homer' said it best:

"There is a time for many words, and there is also time for sleep."

According to Oxford University sleep expert Professor Colin Espie, most people are not getting enough sleep. Professor Espie states:

"The importance of sleep for individual and societal benefit has been almost completely neglected in both policy and practice."

A report that Professor Espie helped to put together called, 'Waking up to the health benefits of sleep', for the Royal Society for Public Health, stated that the UK public is under sleeping by an average of almost an hour every night.

Which over the course of one-week is one whole night worth of sleep deprivation!

The Royal Society for Public Health's study of 2000 UK adults revealed:

- Average sleep time is 6.8 hours, which is below the average of 7.7 hours that most people feel they need.

- 54% of the people in the study felt stressed as a result of poor sleep.

One part of the study certainly increased my level of happiness and made me laugh when it stated:

- One in 20 people have fallen asleep during sex.

Of course you can't simply say that everybody has to have eight hours of sleep and that's the end of the conversation.

Some people won't want to sleep for eight hours; whereas other people feel that they need more than eight hours of sleep to function at their optimal level.

Ultimately, you will know if you're getting enough sleep

because your own body will tell you.

If you're tired and stressed all of the time then you'll have to go to bed a little bit earlier.

The argument against this is that you need to do your work, you need to spend time with the children, you need to do exercise, you need some of your own time, and you also need time for your relationships with people.

This is true for many people, but if you're going through life like a walking zombie, then you're going to have to make getting enough sleep a priority!

If you have to cut 15 minutes off your exercise routine, cut 15 minutes off spending time with a loved one, cut 15 minutes off not spending time with the children or cut 15 minutes off just having some time to yourself, then do it!

However, also find the balance in all areas of your life, rather than cut any areas down too much, or out completely.

Do it for your own sake and for the sake of people around you, because the better you feel, the better your attitude towards others will be.

Of course, this is a complete generalisation, and some

people won't have children, or family members, or they won't want to spend any minute of the day on their own, or they don't do any exercise.

All of that is irrelevant.

Ultimately, what this shows is, whatever you put your time into, you can always cut down certain activities so that you can get an hour more sleep if you feel you need it.

With 24 hours in the day you could say that 6 to 8 of those hours is for sleep, maybe there is eight hours of work and maybe there is eight hours after work until you go to bed.

Again, this is different for everybody.

Some people will want to sleep less, and some want to sleep more.

Some people will want to work more, and some people will work less, and of course, some people will have more free time than others.

People that know me well, know I'm a pretty driven person, but that doesn't mean I'm on the go all the time with lots of energy and enthusiasm.

I also have days where I think, "I can't be bothered to do anything and I'd like to just chill in the garden, on the sofa or lie down on the bed, and maybe read something or watch a movie."

You have to be driven to achieve things, but sometimes you just need to take some rest time and go again when you're feeling fresh.

You'll hear many times throughout some of my books that it does take extra effort to be successful in life, but you have to know the difference between productive extra effort and burning yourself out, in which you're constantly tired and operating on only 80% capacity.

If you're not getting enough sleep and you feel tired all day, you simply won't enjoy life as much, you won't be able to make smart decisions like you can when you're fully recharged and you won't be happy.

Ultimately, make it a priority to get enough sleep because it will lead to a happier and healthier life!

"Sleep is that golden chain that ties health and our bodies together."
Thomas Dekker

Happy

5 – START YOUR DAY OFF RIGHT

"Happiness depends upon ourselves."
Aristotle

Happy

When NASA launches a rocket, they will have put a lot of thought and preparation into it. Also, when they launch the rocket it needs to be going in exactly the right direction.

If a rocket is destined for deep space (which is a starting point of 2 million kilometres away) and is only 1 degree off at the start of its launch, by the time it reaches deep space, it will be thousands of miles off course if it is left unadjusted.

It's important that we start our day off right because the better we start our day off the more likely we are to keep on track with being happy throughout the day.

As we go through our day there will be little challenges that come up that can, if we let them, throw us off course.

So, we need to be constantly adjusting, we need to focus on the big picture and the end goal, while at the same time enjoying all the little things around us that we can be grateful for.

I woke up one morning and was thinking about things that didn't go right for me in the past, which of course is never a good way to start your day.

You may have also done this yourself several times in your life.

As I stood there in my home, I thought, hang on a minute; life is perfect for me right now.

I thought about the present moment:

- I wasn't in any physical pain.

- I had food in my belly.

- I had enough water to drink.

- I was with my son Léon.

So, I changed what I was saying to myself in my head, from what I haven't got, to what I have got, and of course it made me feel better!

You may be in a dark place and think that you haven't got

much going for you.

You may be so focused on what you haven't got that it's clouded your reality, and you can only see the negative things in your life.

If we want to be happy, it's vital that we don't focus on what we haven't got and focus on what we have got!

These could be things like:

- Your family.

- Your health.

- The country you live.

- The time in history you live in.

Think about and write down 10 things that you have got in your life right now:

- ....

- ....

- ....

- ....

- ....

- ....

- ....

- ....

- ....

- ....

Out of these 10 things, which ones could you take out of your life?

Probably not many of them!

So, appreciate them, cherish them, and think about how lucky you are to have certain things in your life.

If you take living in your country for granted, or if you think that people or the government of your country has wronged you in some way, then how would you like to be exported to places such as:

- Iraq
- Afghanistan
- The Congo
- Rwanda
- Sierra Leone

If you're not bothered about the time you live in, let's transport you back to:

- The Dark Ages
- The Stone Age
- World War 1

If you don't care about where you are and the freedom you enjoy, let's transport you back to a place or a time that would have a negative effect on you such as:

- Being a slave
- Nazi Occupation
- Being accused of a crime you didn't commit and sentenced

It's always important to be grateful for what you've got!

FEED YOUR MIND WITH POSITIVITY IN THE MORNING

One of the things I've noticed over the years is that

sometimes I'll be playing a self-development audio and one of my friends, girlfriends or family has heard it and thought that it's a waste of time and all a bit stupid.

Not all high achievers listen to self-development audio or read books, so you don't have to do it to be a success at something.

However, when you go outside of your own beliefs and thoughts, and start listening to other people's experiences and views on things, you then get a much broader perspective of life's situations and it can open your mind up to new possibilities.

Now, this next sentence may seem like bragging, but it isn't, all it is is something I've observed over the years.

The one thing I have noticed with the people who usually shun this habit is that I've never met one of these people who has better mental health than me or are happier than me.

They may be a lot more successful than me in different areas of their life, but in terms of happiness, definitely not!

Some of them may have achieved more in terms of medals or money but most of them seem to struggle more with day-to-day life.

I do know people that are very happy with their lives, but these people don't shun any type of psychological research or personal development.

In every case I've come across, the people that I know that are the happiest have educated themselves throughout the years on the inner workings of the mind, which means they are ahead of 95 to 99% of the population when it comes to mental toughness, happiness and overcoming challenges.

Am I saying that the happiest people I know (myself included) have got everything worked out in their minds and that their minds don't bat an eyelid when things go wrong?

Definitely not!

However, reading and listening to self-development material does give you the ability to bounce back far quicker than you would without it!

"He who learns but does not think, is lost! He who thinks but does not learn, is in great danger."
Confucius

Happy

6 – YOUR HAPPINESS DEPENDS ON YOUR FOCUS

"Happiness depends more on the inward disposition of mind than on outward circumstances."
Benjamin Franklin

Happy

Some people love to wallow in self-pity and get into the habit of having self-defeating emotions every day.

It's much easier for them to wallow in self-pity than to make the effort to pull themselves out of the psychological hole in which they find themselves in!

Even though most people like this won't admit it, they end up in love with feeling sorry for themselves.

At the very least, they are more comfortable in their unhappiness and self-pity, than they are with making a positive change.

Most humans have gone through exactly the same types of feelings, emotions, and negative thoughts, such as feeling:

- Physically in pain
- Psychologically in pain

- Like a loser (when I'm not where I think I should be in life)
- Not loved
- Not wanted
- Rejected
- Lonely
- Sad
- Depressed
- Peeved
- Annoyed
- Pissed off
- Angry
- Jealous
- Wanting revenge
- Unforgiving
- The sense of loss
- Pathetic
- Weak

As well as a whole range of other negative emotions throughout our lives.

Yep, I've been lucky enough, or unlucky enough to experience a broad range of emotions, as I'm sure you have too?

This is good news, because if I was the sort of person that was just happy from the day I was born and nothing ever affected me emotionally, then it would be impossible for you to relate to me, or this book.

We're all human beings, we're all in the same boat together, and the vast majority of us are all built with these of emotions.

Despite having experienced these negative emotions, we can still develop our brains to minimise the affect of these thoughts, and we can subsequently recover a lot quicker by being more aware of them than when we were younger!

Most humans have also gone through exactly the same types of feelings, emotions, and positive thoughts, such as:

- Healthy
- Happy
- In love
- Loved
- Cared for
- Looked after
- Wanted
- Accepted
- Forgiving
- A winner
- Sympathetic

- Empathetic
- Generous
- Mentally strong

The chances are that you're just like me and you've been through pretty much all of these experiences too!

"Regardless of your circumstances, how you feel is mainly down to you, and what you focus on!"

If you're always focusing on the first negative list then you're going to make yourself depressed, but if you choose to focus on your wins in life, and the positive things in your life, whether they are in the past, present, or possibilities for the future, then you're going to be a lot happier!

Most people know that when you feed your body with things that are either high in bad saturated fats or things with a lot of sugar in them, then it's going to have a negative effect on your body in one way or another.

Even if you have one of these metabolisms where you can eat what you want and not put on fat, eating unhealthy food and drinks will have negative effects on your internal body systems.

How you look at things in life will make a massive

difference to your happiness!

I was listening to a great audiobook by James Clear called 'Automatic Habits' and he mentioned that he had heard a story about a man who used a wheelchair and was asked, how does he feel using the wheelchair, because it confined him.

The man replied by saying that it doesn't confine him, it liberates him, as without the wheelchair he would be stuck at home all day and would not be able to get about as much.

Because that was the story he told himself, it made his life a lot easier as mentally he felt better about his situation, which in turn turned him into a happy person.

So, whatever your situation, you need to find a story that eases the mental strain in your head.

One day my son Léon asked me the question, "are you rich Daddy?"

It was a good question, and I had a good think about it before I answered him.

Of course the greatest wealth is your internal wealth, and how good your state of mind and mental health is; but I knew what he meant, so I answered him in terms of money.

I said, "It depends who you compare me to."

Léon replied, "What do you mean Daddy?"

"Well if you compare me to some people I'm not financially rich, but if you compare me to those children in Africa on the TV who are drinking dirty water, I'm extremely rich financially."

I was referring to an advert we had just seen on the TV where the actor, Jeremy Irons, was asking people to donate £3 to Water Aid by sending a text.

I remember listening to a Billy Connolly interview in which he said, "I know billionaires who don't think they're rich."

So, it's all down to how we look at things, and it's always better to focus on the positive than it is to belittle yourself or tell yourself what you haven't got.

Maybe there has been a time in your life when you felt secure in your job and then one day you got told that you were no longer needed… "Hasta la vista baby!"

You think, "oh great, now how am I going to pay for my food, my rent, my mortgage, my car, the gas, the electric, the loans I have?"

It's natural to think about all of those things and you may feel worried.

But we have to remember that,

"It's us that control our thoughts, not the events that happen to us!"

We can decide to interpret situations to our advantage.

I remember losing my job one day and I remember thinking, "shit, I've got no cash!"

But rather than worry myself or my family about what I didn't have, and what I had just lost; I decided to look at this as an opportunity.

In challenging times we need to ask ourselves the right questions.

In a situation like this, a good question to ask yourself is, "have I got more qualifications, wisdom and knowledge now than I did when I left school?"

If the answer is yes, then you have a massive advantage over when you left formal education!

You may say, "but now I have more bills to pay and responsibilities than I did than when I left education."

This is probably true, but would you rather go back to having what you had when you left school?

Many people would not.

On a personal note, I wouldn't like to go back to being 16 again.

Don't get me wrong, I'd like another 30 years extended on my life, but I wouldn't like to have to start from scratch all over again.

I wouldn't have the self-confidence that I now enjoy today.

The great experiences that I have had would not be there.

My knowledge would not be there, and my son would not be here.

Yes, there are other things that would be there, my grandad and uncle (that brought me up), my Siberian

Husky 'Hope' would be there, heck even my hair would be there!

All jokes aside, there are certain things in life that we cannot change, and we have to be grateful for the time we've had with the special people in our lives.

Relationships will come and go, that is the natural way of life.

Whether somebody is taken from us because the relationship has ended, or on not such a great note or whether that person has passed away, people will disappear from our lives.

When I look back at some of my relationships with past girlfriends, rather than being bitter about them, I chose to be grateful for the time I had with them.

At the time of writing (June 2020) I've had five serious relationships in my life: Jo, Laura, Hayley 1 (my Son's mum), Hayley 2, and Ambreen.

Although a few of them may not have ended great (as happens sometimes) I still care about them all and hope they live a great life.

The way I look at things is, when one door closes, another

one opens.

Never let bitter feelings consume you because by holding onto bitterness and negative feelings, the only person this will hurt is you.

As the Buddha said,

"Holding on to anger is like grasping a hot coal with the intent of throwing it at someone else."

Around 50% of marriages fail, and even the ones that don't end up in divorce, it doesn't mean that those couples have a fantastically happy marriage.

God knows how many relationships fail and over 70% of businesses fail, so if you try something and it doesn't work out, then don't worry. You're not alone!

Just because the thing you tried failed, doesn't mean you're a failure!

When adversity hits, you can look at it in the 'poor me' way, or you can think about what a great opportunity it is to show the world that you're a winner, no matter what happens!

I never look back at a job I didn't stay in, or a relationship

I didn't stay in, as a failure.

Each one was a success for a certain period of time and I'm grateful for everything that I've experienced.

How do you think that affects me mentally?

It's pretty obvious, it makes me very happy, and you can do exactly the same thing too.

If you want to live the happy and fulfilled life you want, the only way forward is to focus on the positive things in your life!

Happy

7 – MAKE PEOPLE HAPPY

"Try to be a rainbow in someone's cloud."
Maya Angelou

Happy

Making other people happy can add to your own happiness, but it's important you are also happy.

If you are making a lot of other people happy and you feel empty and unhappy in yourself, then it's because you're focusing on what you think you're lacking or you're not grateful for.

As Dodinsky said,

"Be there for others, but never leave yourself behind."

One day, I was sitting in my car outside the supermarket waiting for my mum to come out and I noticed a lady who was smiling, laughing, and interacting with other people.

This lady wasn't stunningly beautiful, in fact she didn't even have the best physique, but what she did have is an incredible personality.

As I watched this lady at the checkout I thought to myself how wonderful it was as I could see that she was a ray of sunshine in what is normally not the most joyous of places.

I thought to myself how grateful I am to have people in my life who are happy and make me feel better.

In life you can get two types of people.

1. The type of person that brightens up the room when he or she walks into the room.

2. The type of person that brightens up the room when he or she walks out of the room.

It's important to make an effort (because sometimes it does take an effort) to have a positive effect on other people's lives.

Nobody wants to be around doom and gloom all the time because it will drag you down as well!

When you go out of your way to pay a compliment to somebody or to try and lighten up somebody's day, you make a difference in a person's life.

The chances are if it's a stranger, you won't know what's

going on in that person's life, but everybody in life is fighting a battle, and some are fighting harder battles than others.

Even as I sit here writing these words, a man rode past me in his wheelchair, and I can see that he is in his 70s, and he has only one leg.

As he goes around the back of my car, another car is blocking my view so I can no longer see this elderly gentleman in the wheelchair.

I decide to go out and see if I can help with anything, but fortunately somebody is already there and looking after him.

At some point in our lives we are all going to need help from people.

It doesn't matter if you're super-duper tough, or you're worth billions of pounds.

At some point, you will need somebody else to take the load off of your day.

We can't be there for everyone, but we can help some people some of the time.

When you make a difference in other people's lives you may not think much of it at the time, but the more you can make a difference in other people's lives, the more value you add to the community, and the more your own self-worth will grow.

As Martin Luther King Jr said,

"Life's most persistent and urgent question is, what are you doing for others?"

Whilst I was waiting again outside the supermarket and jotting down my thoughts, I had a little tap on my car. When I looked up, I could see Helmut, a local taxi driver looking at me and smiling.

Helmut's originally from Germany and when we met, we started talking about what a beautiful place Germany is as several years before, I had been to a part of Germany called Bavaria to visit the Neuschwanstein Castle.

Neuschwanstein Castle is a beautiful fairytale type looking palace that the Chief Designer at Disney, Herbert Dickens Ryman, is said to have modelled the Cinderella's Castle in Disney's Magic Kingdom from.

Helmut asked me how things were going, and I told him overall they were going really well, even though I had just broken up with my girlfriend.

"Oh" he said, and then went silent.

After somebody says words like that about a relationship break-up, with a boyfriend or girlfriend, the other person expects something negative to come out of your mouth.

However, I replied that I had parked my car down at the supermarket carpark so I could just watch hot girls go in and out all day long!

Helmut didn't expect me to say that and he burst out laughing!

Of course, I was just saying it for a joke, okay I was kind of half-joking but seeing him laugh also made me feel better.

As our conversation carried on, he told me that he loved seeing things that I had been doing for certain people.

So, I had made him feel good by complementing the country that he came from, and also by telling him that I was now the town's local pervert looking at beautiful women.

Helmut also made me feel good by telling me about the

other good things I had been doing in the community.

The point of the story is, if you go out of your way to help people and make people feel better about themselves, the chances are they will return those feelings back to you.

Of course there are times when you are nice to people and they are not nice back, but most of the time, if you send good vibes out to people, then good vibes will come back to you.

You've probably done the same sort of thing yourself.

You've probably complimented someone and made them feel good, and in doing this, you feel good about yourself.

Even if they didn't compliment you back on something that you had done, there is a very good chance you would still have enjoyed sending out positive vibes to them.

So make others happy and it will help make you happier!

"Spread the love everywhere you go. Let no one ever come to you without leaving happier."
Mother Teresa

8 – THE HAPPIEST COUNTRIES

Happy

Right, it's time to get political! Nah, only joking, but it needs to be said that Governments too can play a part in our happiness because laws and legislation affect our lives.

- Freedom
- Wealth
- Starting wars
- Poverty
- Ethnic cleansing
- Communism
- Democracy
- Taking responsibility and control of your life

I'm not going to go into the politics of the list above because that isn't what this book is about.

All I'm going to do is point out a few things that governments can control to various degrees.

In 2017, a report was published listing the happiest countries in the world.

The world happiness report ranked countries on six different factors, they were:

- Freedom
- Caring
- Generosity
- Honesty
- Income
- Health

Norway came out top!

Many experts believe that it came out on top because of high life expectancy, high levels of gender equality, very good healthcare, high GDP per capita, very good education and not to mention it's beautiful landscape!

Author and columnist Eric Dregni lived in Norway for one year and studied there for three years.

After he heard about the list, he decided to go back to Norway, talk to people and see if he could find some clues as to why as a nation, they seemed to be happier than most.

Dregni said, "Inger Brøgger Bull, a librarian from Oslo, didn't understand why Norway was ranked as the happiest country in the world."

She said, "we have bad weather, the highest prices for beer, things are so expensive!"

However, it turns out that Norwegians use the word 'we' a lot more than they use the word 'I.'

In many societies around the world it's more about 'ME, ME, ME' and what can I achieve, whereas Norwegians in general, focused more on everybody doing well in life!

For me, this was an important part of the survey and it meant a lot to me, simply because I have a very similar mindset, and I do sincerely believe that helping other people and caring about them plays a massive part in my happiness.

Even when people don't like me, or don't want me to do well, I still wish them all the best!

I know that sounds a little bit crazy, but the way I see it is, people have to deal with their own problems, and I haven't got time to worry about what they are thinking about and it should be the same with you.

If you worry too much about what people think about you, it can be detrimental to your happiness.

What people think about you has no direct effect on the way you feel and think if you decide to not let it bother you!

(I cover this more in my book 'No F*cks Given' which is due to be released in the later part of 2020).

One Norwegian also said,

"I think perhaps we Norwegians have become a bit smug, since we consider ourselves so peaceful and helpful. It's not so nice when Norway considers itself a bit better than other places."

When I read that paragraph I had to question it, because what's wrong with considering yourself peaceful and helpful?

I can see why the Norwegian said, 'we may be a bit smug about that,' but my feelings on it personally, is that he should be proud of that.

"If you consider yourself more peaceful and helpful than the majority of people, then that makes you a better person, which in turn will make the world a better

place."

As I continued to read the article, his wife Inger said,

"Openness to helping others is the essence of Norway's success. We have a willingness to give a part of ourselves for the whole."

That's powerful stuff!

Some of the other things on the list that many Norwegians considered valuable was being free in nature.

Everyone has a right to roam free in Norway!

According to the documentary, no one 'absolutely' owns the land, which means anyone can come and camp on people's land for the night, and all that is expected of you is to clean up at the end of your stay.

This is obviously a little different to many countries, as farmers wouldn't take too kindly to a lot of people camping on their land.

I have a scenario in my head of an angry farmer chasing a happy hippy weed smoking camper with a pitchfork!

I think back in the day, some farmers would have come

out brandishing their 12 bore shotguns!

Employers in Norway are required to give employees at least 25 days of paid annual holiday, and they want their employees to enjoy it.

Even though Norway hit the top of the list in 2017, when I first researched this piece the country that had won the 'Happiest Country in The World' title the most times was Denmark (at the time of editing in 2020).

Ultimately, it's the Scandinavian countries that always rank highest in the World Happiness Report.

When it comes to paying taxes, 9 out of 10 Danish people will say that they are happily paying their taxes because they know it is going to benefit not only themselves, but also their community and their friends.

Norwegians trust their government to spend their taxes in ways that will hugely benefit the country and their community.

It seems that many Danish people are happy because they have guaranteed free child day care, free health care and a top-notch education system.

One of the main reasons for the higher overall happiness

in Scandinavian countries, is that they are grateful for what the have got.

There's that word 'grateful' again, that seems to pop up all the time when it comes to happiness.

When I went to Denmark, I visited Copenhagen.

Copenhagen is one of the worlds most environmentally conscious cities, in which over a third of people ride bikes.

Rates of poverty, unemployment and homelessness are extremely low.

In Denmark, most schooling is free (which is the same as many rich countries) and when Danes go to university, they get some money to contribute towards their undergraduate education.

An American reporter visited Denmark and asked a Dane called Peter Morgensen a few questions.

Morgensen is an economist and chief political editor of Denmark's second largest newspaper, Politiken.

The reporter asked him, "How many Danes experience financial distress, or lose their homes, or go bankrupt because they get sick?"

Morgensen gave the American reporter a puzzled look and said to him, "why none of course" (because of government support for people).

The Dane was genuinely baffled by the question, because to him, it was ridiculous to think that anyone would lose their house or go bankrupt because of medical bills.

The reporter explained to Morgensen that every year millions of Americans lose their homes or go bankrupt because of medical bills.

The reporter went on to say that half of all bankruptcies in the United States are caused by people being sick.

Morgensen also told the reporter that in Denmark they couldn't imagine living like that.

The American reporter went on to say that one of the big reasons that the Danish are happier than Americans (in this example) generally, is because the Danish government supports parents massively when they have children.

American women receive an average of 10.3 weeks for maternity leave.

In Denmark, new mothers receive an average of 52 weeks parental leave and their salary paid for by the government (which obviously came from the taxes that most Danes happily contributed towards).

The rest of the paid time off can be divided by the family.

Denmark also consistently ranks as one of the best countries in the world for gender equality.

The gender pay gap is also substantially less in Denmark than in the US.

In Denmark, the gap between the richest people and the poorest people is one of the smallest gaps in the world.

The reason for the low levels of inequality links to the fact that the average middle-class Dane pays (at the time of writing) between 45% and 53% in taxes, while the wealthiest Dane's pay over 60% in taxes.

The poorest Dane's that are payed under $31,000 a year pay 30% taxes.

According to many surveys, Denmark has the best work/life balance in the world.

Social problems and bad health are far worse in countries with less equality.

In almost all the statistics from infant mortality, to mental illness, to teenage pregnancy, and to murder; it seems that the more equal a country is, the level of crime is lower, mental illness is lower, along with a whole list of other things.

Scandinavians generally take things in their stride far more than many other nationalities. Especially, a lot more than people who live in busy cities and succumb to 'the rat race', you know, the people who haven't got the time to talk because they're too busy being quote/unquote "busy."

One of the other things that stood out in the reports was that Scandinavians have a general respect for their fellow citizens.

In other words, they treat other people like they would like to be treated.

Scandinavians also have a very strong belief in the power of their community.

European countries such as Sweden, Austria, Switzerland, Germany, Norway, Luxembourg, and Denmark are not only normally in the top 10 happiest places in the world, but they also consistently rank in the top 10 countries in the world with the lowest crime rates.

I've been lucky enough to travel to all of those countries I just mentioned, and there is no doubt that I felt completely safe wherever I was.

America is one of my favourite countries on this earth, however there are so many places in America where you wouldn't find me in the early hours of the morning, simply because it's too dangerous.

Although much of western media reports that Africans are poor but happy, the reality is a little different.

I've been to Africa and I can say that I've met many happy Africans, but in general most of them would rather be in a country like the UK or other 'developed' countries.

In 2020, the happiest country in the world for the world happiness report was Finland.

Even though it fluctuated from country to country such as Norway, Denmark, and Finland one thing is pretty clear for us to see.

Every country that has topped the world happiness report is a Scandinavian country.

People in the UK can look at their country and think to themselves, but we have the biggest empire in history, we've got all of the most glorious kings and queens.

The Romans can look at their proud history and the Americans often come and say that they live in the greatest country in the world.

The reality is quite different on the world level though.

When you say your country is the best, or you are the best, our ego or patriotism takes over.

Many people are blinded and just believe what they hear.

There is nothing wrong with being proud about your own nationality. I'm incredibly proud to be British, and I wouldn't change it for anything.

I love our heritage, our history, many of our great leaders and high achievers, our National Health System, and our democracy.

There is so much that I love about living in Great Britain.

However, I do believe that a 'we' culture, like that of Scandinavia, is a more natural way of dealing with the stresses and strains of daily life!

Ultimately, no matter what country we live in we have to

do the best with what we've been given and be grateful for it.

Happy

9 – THE HAPPIEST ENVIRONMENT

"You become like the five people you spend the most time with. Choose carefully."
Jim Rohn

Happy

Several years ago when my son Léon was younger, I came across one of the 'Mr Men' books and thought it would be a good idea to introduce Léon to some of the 'Mr Men' characters.

As a child I had many fun memories of being read to or reading 'Mr Men' books.

Some of my favourites were 'Mr Happy', 'Mr Strong', and 'Mr Tickle' so I decided to buy a 'Mr Happy' book for my son and read it to him.

So the story goes a little bit like this:

One day, 'Mr Happy' goes for a walk and comes across a tree with the door.

He opens the door, walks down a set of stairs, and opens another door.

And what does he find when he's opened the other door?

He finds someone who looks exactly like him!

Yes, a big round, yellow looking human/creature or whatever you want to call 'Mr Happy's' character.

However, there was one significant difference between this character and 'Mr Happy,' and that was, rather than smiling, this character had a very unhappy face!

It was 'Mr Miserable!'

'Mr Happy' then asked 'Mr Miserable,' "how would you like to be happy just like me?"

And not in exactly the same words, 'Mr Miserable' says something to the effect of, "yeah I'm up for a bit of that!"

So 'Mr Happy' decides to take 'Mr Miserable' from his house and takes him to where he lives, 'Happy Land.'

After a while of living in Happy Land, 'Mr Miserable' gradually started to smile and become happy himself.

'Mr Miserable' even started to laugh, which in turn, made 'Mr Happy' laugh too.

'Mr Miserable' and 'Mr Happy' then went outside and continued to laugh until their sides hurt, they laughed until their eyes watered and they just kept on laughing.

When other people passed them by, it would make them laugh too.

Shit, even the birds in the trees started to laugh!

Well, I'm sure that you felt all warm and gooey inside about that beautiful little story didn't you?

But all jokes aside, the great thing about this little story is that there is a lot of truth to it.

If you're in an environment where you have consistently been unhappy, then you need to take your ass out of that environment!

You not only need to take yourself out of that environment, you need to be around happy and positive people who can lift your spirits; when you do that, you will indeed become a happier person!

However, you have to decide to be happy!

If you consistently want to be a grumpy bastard, and that is the vision you have of yourself, and that is the life you want to lead, then fine, you can stay grumpy.

Some people are happy being grumpy. Sounds a bit weird, but these people seem to enjoy being a grumpy and unhappy person because it's what they are comfortable with.

The most important thing is to be around good people who add some positive value to your life.

It's not just about associating with high achievers, because some high achievers may have a completely different set of values to you, and if that's the case, it would be soul destroying to be around people (no matter what their status), who do things that you feel very uncomfortable with.

You need to be around happy positive people, who like to help others and haven't got the world's allocation of dramas in their lives.

You've probably come across this type of person before.

Everything that happens in their lives is blown out of all proportion and boy do they like to have a song and dance about it!

You know it's the type of person who always says, "I don't

suffer fools gladly."

Little do they realise they only need to look into the mirror to see who the real fool is.

They are the type of person who is operating on a very low level of consciousness, in other words, they can only ever see things from their perspective and to hell with how you feel.

They also like to play the victim in life all the time, if you've had it tough, they've had it tougher, and they'll be the first person to tell you about it!

If you have this type of person in your life, then your life is going to be a pile of dramas and very unpleasant situations, in short…your life will be a pile of shit.

It doesn't matter how healthy you are, it doesn't matter how much you achieve, it doesn't matter how much money you have, if you're around this type of person long enough, they will turn your life into a steaming pile of cow poop!

We all know someone like that, but if you've got this type of person as one of your friends, and you're in touch with them every day, then I suggest you back off and spend your time somewhere else.

If your partner is this type of person and won't change their ways, that's like them being the iceberg and you're the Titanic.

In other words you're heading for a crash and you'll be on the way down if you don't change course.

I don't care how positive or how motivated you are, if you're around a poisonous person all the time, your mental state will take a turn for the worst.

I can't stress enough how important it is to be around the right people!

10 – BEING KIND TO PEOPLE

"Be kind, for everyone you meet is fighting a hard battle."
Plato

Happy

The type of people that I like the most are the ones that are down-to-earth and kind to people.

They treat people as they would like to be treated.

When you're kind to people, the chances are, they're going to be kind back to you.

However, this doesn't always work in life.

Sometimes, you get people that want to take advantage of your kind nature; I know first-hand, as years ago I got bullied a bit.

I was never nasty to those people or rude to them, but they decided to take it upon themselves to be complete twats to me!

Looking back, maybe I should've just hit the person and win or lose, it could have stopped their bullying, which is what I did with somebody when I was around 16 years old.

The guy kept on punching me in the arm for no reason and giving me a nasty look, and this happened several times until I got to the stage where I'd had enough of it and told a friend that I was going to have a fight with him.

My friend went and told the bully that I said I was going to fight him, so the bully decided to come over to me, grab my hair and say, "I hear that you wanted a fight with me?"

I knew that I might as well just go for it, so I dropped the head on him and fortunately won the fight.

He never bullied me after that.

That challenge with the other bullies was that it was mainly in army training, and I was scared of getting thrown out of the service.

They were both a higher rank than me and loved by the Sergeant who was also a complete asshole and a bully!

I was classed as a 'nobody' back then in my troop and if I got kicked out for fighting it would be no loss to anyone apart from myself.

My confidence was very low back then, and I thought that if I was kicked out for fighting, I'd struggle to get another job, and my life would be one massive struggle and completely boring.

Some people that are bullied can turn into bullies themselves but doing that always works against you in the long run.

Being kind is the way ahead not only for other people, but for us too!

Just doing little things like letting somebody out when they're stuck in traffic, or holding the door open for somebody, will make that person happier and you should also feel good for doing it.

I was staying in a hotel one evening and as I was walking through the reception area, on the way to my room, I noticed an intoxicated woman being extremely rude to one of the male receptionists.

He had done nothing personally wrong to gain the wrath of this woman; all he had done was be in the wrong place at the wrong time.

Later on that evening, I ended up going back to reception when the woman had gone.

I had a chat to the guy at reception and said to him, "don't worry about that she's just had too much to drink and none of that is your fault."

I could see that he was still a bit shook up by the whole situation, and I wanted to do something that would help counter his negative feelings.

I needed my clothes ironed for the next day so I asked him if he could bring an iron to my room and I also asked if he could bring some sweeteners as well for my coffee.

Within the next 5 to 10 minutes he came up with the iron and the requested handful of sweeteners.

I thanked him for this, and I said to him, "do you believe that out of every bad situation comes a positive situation?"

He wasn't from the UK, and I didn't know how well he spoke English, but he kind of looked on in bewilderment at my question, so I said to him, "I believe that good things can come from negative situations," and with that, I went over to my desk in my room got a £10 note and gave it to him as a tip.

He said that there was no need to give him a tip, but I just said take it and have a great evening.

I could see that he appreciated the tip and I knew that it was a ray of light on his dampened spirits.

In all honesty I can say that I felt quite good for giving him the £10, but at the same time I did think to myself it's not about how I feel, my main goal was to make him feel a little bit better and a little bit happier.

If you can be a ray of light in somebody's life, whether it's a small gesture or something big, it can really make a difference to people's lives!

There's no losing in a situation like this, the chances are, you'll feel good about what you've done, and the chances are, they're going to feel a little bit better about you having come into their life and showing kindness towards them.

If you want to gain more happiness in your life then it's always a good idea to make other people happy.

However, there are some people who make other people happy that aren't happy themselves.

A typical example of this are some comedians.

There are many comedians out there who make it their life's work to lighten peoples load in life and make other people happy through their comedy.

Sadly, some comedians hit some very dark times.

Of course there are a couple of obvious people that we can think of, one being Robin Williams, who sadly took his own life.

Jim Carrey also went through a time in which he was very depressed and struggled with life.

So, making other people happy doesn't always make yourself happy, this goes back to the thoughts you say to yourself.

Being more famous or having more money doesn't necessarily create happiness, as we know.

There are countless examples of celebrities that have gone through a very dark period in their lives.

If you were to ask me which one book I consider the best book I've ever read in my life, the book that really comes to mind is Dale Carnegie's, 'How to Win Friends and Influence People.'

Getting on in this world has a lot to do with how well you get on with other people, and if you're looking for a book on how to master people skills, be influential and get what you want then this is a great book to read.

When it comes to getting certain things in life, it's always a good idea to give before you receive.

One of the things I always try to do to the best of my ability is to give value to other people.

Even with this book, I want to give value, and even if just one sentence in this book helps you in some way in life, I know that this book will have achieved its purpose.

Many authors have a dream of being a bestseller, which is cool and everything, but for me, it's never really about that, it's more about helping people in some way.

Yes, all of these other achievements and accolades are always a nice little bonus but for me, it's not the main purpose of this book.

One of the little side bonuses of helping a person is it can be very beneficial to your mental health.

Many people know that exercise is an excellent way to feel good about yourself and stay positive, but sadly, all too often these days, the doctor will prescribe pills for somebody who's feeling down and going through a bad patch. In my experience however, we need to try other options first.

I haven't covered exercise in depth in this book because it's something that I'll cover in other books.

One of the major benefits of being nice and sincere to people is it is very good for your mental health.

If you're a bit rude and arrogant, sometimes that can come back and bite you on the bum.

It might even get to the stage when you think 'poor old me.'

However, you may be able to trace your behaviour back and see that you caused a lot of the problems that you now have.

"Three things in human life are important.
The first is to be kind.
The second is to be kind.
And the third is to be kind."
Henry James

11 – YOUR PERSONAL CHEERLEADERS

"No individual can win a game by himself."
Pele

Happy

An experiment conducted by a TV show called 'Brain Games', on the National Geographic Channel, showed a woman who tried to get a basketball through a net and was given 10 shots.

There was also a crowd of approximately 15 volunteers standing and watching her.

When she started missing the shots, the crowd sent out negative vibes towards her.

The first time she attempted the 10 shots she didn't score any baskets and felt emotionally deflated, as not only was she missing the shots, but the crowd were not supportive and very dismissive of her.

She was then blindfolded, and while standing at the same place where she previously shot from, she tried to score two baskets with two shots with the blindfold on.

However, the difference was this time, she had a crowd there cheering her on.

When she threw the first ball, the crowd cheered and told her she had scored a basket (when in reality, the shot was way off the basket).

Of course, she was delighted with this so, still blindfolded, she tried with a second shot, and again, the crowd cheered her as if she had scored a basket twice in a row which lifted her spirits massively!

She believed she was scoring baskets even though she wasn't!

She was feeling pretty good about herself at this point and was asked to take another 10 shots without a blindfold on.

This was the same as what she had first done, but this time the crowd were totally behind her and really supportive, even when she missed the basket.

She missed the first shot, and she also missed the second shot, but the crowd was still totally supportive of her.

Even though she was missing the basket, she was a lot closer to scoring than when the crowd wasn't supporting her.

On her third attempt, she threw the ball and it went straight through the net.

Everybody, including herself, was delighted with this and it gave her a huge psychological boost!

On her fourth attempt, she threw the ball and it hit the rim of the basket, not once but twice, and then incredibly, the ball bounced through the net!

Again, she was delighted!

The crowd had big smiles on their faces; they were clapping their hands and were showing total support for her.

The Presenter of Brain Games said afterwards:

"Wow! By making her think she sank those blindfolded shots, and by cheering and giving positive reinforcement, it's almost like we hacked her self-confidence and got her to believe more in her natural abilities."

Amazingly, she scored 4 out of 10 baskets, which was a huge improvement from her 0 out of 10 shots.

They also conducted another experiment in which they got a good basketball player, called Josh, who (not blindfolded) scored 9 out of 10 baskets.

The experiment wanted to know if there was anything that the people around him could do to make him a worse player.

Josh then had to put a blindfold on and was asked to take one shot.

When the presenter said to the crowd, "do you think he can do it guys?"

The crowd replied very negatively and said, "no."

Josh had a smile on his face even though the crowd responded negatively and then stood at the line ready to throw his first shot blindfolded.

When he took the shot he missed it, but (unlike the crowd from the girl that wasn't as good with her initial shots), the crowd sent out negative vibes his way.

The negative vibes weren't aggressive, but they were very unsupportive, and he knew they didn't believe that he could do it.

The TV presenter said to him, "not quite, but it's okay, let him try a second time."

Josh threw the second shot, again he missed, and again the crowd sent out negative vibes, booed and said "no."

In all fairness, from the outside Josh still had a smile on his face and didn't look too discouraged.

The presenter then asked Josh to take off his blindfold and said,

"So listen, it wasn't as easy as we thought, but let's have you do 10 throws again without the blindfold. Do your thing, 9 out of 10, maybe 10 out of 10."

As Josh stood to throw his first basket the crowd still weren't supportive of him, and when they were asked by the presenter if they thought he'd get a basket, they said "no."

Josh threw the first shot and scored a basket, but even though he scored, the crowd was still negative and booing.

At this point, you could see that the crowd had got to Josh mentally!

On the second shot, the crowd were booing him, and Josh missed the shot with the ball bouncing off the outer rim of the basket.

Josh was still smiling, but you could see that he was also deflated.

On his third shot, he missed again, whereas before without the crowd's negativity, he scored 9 out of 10 shots.

On the fourth attempt, he also missed and fell short!

The crowd kept saying negative things and in the end, Josh only made 5 out of 10 baskets, which was four down from his average before.

Josh was very good compared to the average person; he certainly wasn't a professional but the negative people around him severely affected his performance!

They did 'the positive crowd' and 'the negative crowd' experiment on many other people and for the most part the result was the same.

When people were supporting and cheering the person trying to score the basket, the player performed on a higher level; when the crowd were negative and unsupportive, the players generally performed on a poor level!

However, there were a minority of people that still managed to score high on a consistent level even when the people were booing and unsupportive of them.

When they were asked how they had the ability to do that, one of the women said that she used to play college basketball and was used to people booing and reacting in a negative way.

In other words, she had trained her brain to a higher level and part of getting to that higher level was focusing and not being rocked by the negativity that was around her!

Most of the best professional basketball players will focus so intensely and believe in themselves so much, that even if the crowd were booing them, they would still perform at a high standard!

But this can affect professional players too.

If you've ever watched any sports match on TV, you'll know that when a team plays a home game they are more likely to win.

Yes, they may be more familiar with the ground, but even more important than that is the support from the fans, which gives them more of a psychological boost and helps them perform better.

In fact there are many high achievers that use this

negative psychology to spur them on.

Michael Jordan was arguably the greatest basketball player in history. He was one of these people that used negativity from others to drive him on mentally to help him become the success that he was.

Whenever Michael Jordan had bad press or somebody would personally challenge him, he would rise to the challenge and make a point of thrashing the pants off them!

In fact, people that knew Michael, always said that you should never challenge him, because the chances are, he's going to kick your ass!

We need to do the same thing in life!

Many times there will be the naysayers and doubters in your life, but rather than let that affect you in a negative way, use it as fuel to succeed!

I can tell you from personal experience that I have a lot of people that want to see me go down in flames, which has ironically made me succeed more in life!

So, if I can make that happen, you can too!

However, Michael and other professional team players still have a team around them and fans around them that want them to win.

So, if you have someone that is constantly tearing you down and not supporting you, then you have to make plans to remove them from your life before they grind you down with their unsupportive, negative bullshit!

"Get around people that support you."

With some people, you can give them a pass once or twice if they've been through a difficult situation and said some unkind things to you.

However, it's best to play it like a yellow card if they are constantly nagging at you or being horrible in some way.

If this continues for a long enough period of time, eventually, you need to give them a red card so that they're out of your life!

Most of the time, a substitute will come in and fill the gap in your life that the negative person left, but even if they don't,

"You are strong enough to go forward
without them on your own!"

Happy

12 – BEING GRATEFUL

*"Do not spoil what you have by desire in what you have not;
remember that what you now have was once among the things
you only hoped for."*
Epicurus

Happy

Roman statesman and philosopher Marcus Tullius Cicero (more commonly known as simply 'Cicero') who was one of Rome's greatest orators, described 'gratitude' as the 'mother of all human feelings!'

And according to positivepsychology.com

"It is not happiness that brings us gratitude. It is gratitude that brings us happiness."

There is also peer reviewed scientific research that shows that gratitude actually does the following things to our bodies:

1. Releases toxic emotions

2. Reduces pain

3. Improves sleep quality

4. Aids in stress regulation

5. Reduces anxiety

6. Reduces depression

Léon once said to me, "Daddy would you sell everything in this house for £50,000?"

I stopped and thought about it for a few seconds and said, "I wouldn't sell you."

He said, "No, I mean all of the things in the house like the TV, the laptop, the iPad, the phones etc."

Of course this was quite easy to decide, as every item was not worth as much as £50,000 so I would've gone with the £50k.

However, if somebody offered you £50,000 to get rid of your phone, laptop, tablet, TV, bed, chairs, forever and you could never have them back and you couldn't replace them, would you do it?

Many people, including myself wouldn't.

The reason being, on a personal note, if I got rid of my Samsung smart phone, my iPad, my laptop, and my TV etc, it would be much more difficult to do my work and I could spend the £50k in a relatively short space of time.

Also, to be without a phone or the other devices that we enjoy everyday is something that most people (unless you're a hermit living in a cave) wouldn't opt in for.

I talk about being grateful in some of my other books and I will continue to talk about it in future books too! The reason? Because

"Being grateful is everything when it comes to happiness!"

In fact if you're not grateful it's very difficult to experience true happiness.

In 2013, I moved into a spacious house with my girlfriend in one of the nicest areas in town.

My fitness training was almost non-existent I just did a few bits here and a few bits there.

I had a fairly good income, with a nice sports car and a fast motorbike parked in the drive.

I got comfortable and was drifting along in a fairly easy job. I worked as a support worker and did things like take people with epilepsy, brain injuries, learning difficulties, and autism to the cinema and played games of pool and went for walks with them.

I was a nightclub bouncer, which was also pretty easy.

Most of the time was spent watching people and talking to people every now and again, and every so often, myself and my fellow bouncers would break up a fight.

When I worked in the pubs there wasn't fighting guaranteed on a weekly basis, but in the nightclubs, it was kicking off more often than not.

My other job was doing a little bit of personal training, which normally involved running or power walking.

It's so easy to get caught up in the whole yeah but I'm too fat, too broke, too ugly, too old, too young, not smart enough, not tall enough, not short enough, I don't have the contacts etc...

It's true that there are certain things you're born with that you may not be able to change, but your thinking isn't one of them! So, feed your mind with positive thoughts.

Feed it with fun, with laughter, with inspiration, with quality people, who will genuinely build you up!

So, always visualise yourself being successful because you already are successful at many things.

Think about all of those people that are actually dying from starvation and other diseases that the super rich people in the western world don't have to worry about.

When I say super rich, I mean someone that earns about £10,000 a year, because that is super rich compared to several billion people around the world!

In the UK we've got it even better to some extent in that, you can walk through a wooded area or you can lift up a piece of wood without worrying about a snake biting you and killing you!

After all, we don't have to worry about deadly spiders or frogs, or alligators and crocodiles seriously screwing up your day!

There are no dingoes to take our babies away, no wolves to hunt us down, no lions and tigers and bears 'oh my' that will maul the living crap out of you!

I was lying in bed next to a girlfriend one evening and she read out a quote from a fairly well known entrepreneur who rose to prominence over the past few years through his YouTube channel and the global publication of his books.

The quote was a good one, but one of the things I've noticed about certain people in the quote/unquote 'world of personal achievement' is some (but not all) take themselves and life far too seriously!

Of course when you want to achieve certain goals you have to take them seriously, but when all that matters is the next goal, the next award, or the next mighty dollar then it's easy to stop enjoying life and stop being grateful.

I've seen many people get so consumed in achieving their goals, regardless of anything else, that they risk losing any form of fun in their lives!

Some people have a belief that everyone should follow 'their way' and with that, the fun can vaporise for them too!

As a result, those that develop this tunnel vision will go on to suffer from mental health issues like, stress and anxiety.

So, no matter what goals you are achieving, have fun and be grateful for what you have got!

13 – MONEY MONEY MONEY

*"Happiness resides not in possessions, and not in gold,
happiness dwells in the soul."*
Democritus

Happy

If happiness is all about getting 'things' then everybody in the western world should be ecstatic because what we have compared to billions of people in developing countries is quite shocking.

There are many millionaires that are happy and live a very gifted life. But I'll never forget meeting a guy who told me he was worth £3 million but all he wanted was £6 million.

It's always cool to be striving for new goals, but when your happiness depends on that goal you aren't heading down a dark path, you're already in the dark!

You must decide to be happy right now:

- Not when you become single
- Not when you've got the perfect partner
- Not when you get a divorce
- Not when you get married
- Not when the children leave home

- Not when you have children
- Not when you retire
- Not when you get a new job
- Not when you leave your job
- Not when you've hit a certain fitness goal
- Not when you lose a certain amount of weight
- Not when you put on a certain amount of weight
- Not when you have a certain amount of cash in the bank
- Not for any reason

DECIDE TO BE HAPPY RIGHT NOW!

You can have it two ways: you can be happy now and strive towards your goal, or you can be unhappy until you reach your goal of weighing a certain amount or having £6 million in the bank, like that guy I spoke to.

Ironically, he didn't realise that when he finally hits his target of £6 million he will probably be happy for a few minutes and then be unhappy because he wants £9 million to make him happy.

It's quite funny when you think about what he's doing; it's not that he's stupid, it's just that he's lost track of what success really is.

Most people believe that people's happiness and the

quality of their lives boil down to monetary wealth. There is no doubt that money can help you greatly in your life, but the quality of your psychological wellbeing is not down to how much cash you have in the bank.

There are people who live in the slums of Mumbai who are not happy, there are people in the developed world, who are financially rich in comparison, that live an average life and are not happy.

There are also millionaires and billionaires who are not happy.

By the same token, there are people who live in the slums and people in the developed world who live an average life, as well as millionaires and billionaires who are happy.

I interviewed multimillionaire Alfie Best and asked him if money makes you happy. Alfie is a Romani gypsy that has built up his caravan park empire from nothing.

The last estimated value of Alfie's net worth was over £300 million.

Alfie replied that money can give you a level of comfort, but it doesn't make you happy all the time.

Money can move you to a better neighbourhood, away

from people who bring drama into your life and it definitely gives you a lot more options.

So, have you ever thought that where you live can have an impact on your happiness?

In the UK, there was a popular daytime TV show called 'The Jeremy Kyle Show'.

The producers for the show would find people from the lowest income areas and invite them to become guests in exchange for talking about sleeping with their partners sister or their husbands Dad, or whatever else the crazy ass situation is!

The truth is that in many (but not all) low-income areas, there is more crime, there are more challenges, more mental health issues, more depression, and also more drug use.

One of my heroes in the personal development world was Zig Ziglar.

He was 'a good ol' boy' (as he would have described himself) from Alabama.

Zig was overweight and struggling in life and through the power of changing his mindset, he became one of the most successful self-development authors and motivational speakers in the world.

I have seen how people in the self-development industry and high achievers from all different walks of life, can become such workaholics that their work comes before anything else in life.

Trying to find a balance between making enough money for your family and spending enough time with your family can be a challenging thing to do.

Only a very small percentage of people seem to pull off making good money and spending enough time with loved ones...Zig Ziglar was one of those people!

I remember listening to a speech he did where he said that he was not the best motivational speaker in the world because if he put that much time into speaking, it would come at a high price, and that price was not investing time with his family.

For me personally, it put him in a higher league than many speakers and authors who are constantly on the road chasing the money and recognition at the expense of not seeing their family, or at the expense of not having downtime on their own, or with friends and loved ones.

There is a danger that by being so focused and obsessed with a certain goal, you can lose something far more important – time with the people you love and truly care about!

Although I have many ambitions and goals, I'm also aware that I need to have a balance and it's something I recommend you keep an eye on with your own life too.

If you have the mindset that you'll be happy only when you've got a certain thing in your life, whether that's a handbag, a car, a new man, a new woman, a boat, a watch, a holiday, you're literally wasting your life. You're wasting Life!

I'm not dismissing getting things either, because certain things can make you happier.

For example, if you really enjoyed whatever product you bought then that's great, but your happiness shouldn't depend on these material things!

Getting additional 'things' should just be a tiny little bonus.

When I was a child, I used to love playing with toys such as my 'He-Man' figures or 'Star Wars' models.

I used to love going out on my bike, and I would put a little piece of cardboard next to the spokes with a peg on the bike's metal frame, so that it would make a sound like a motorbike.

Of course it didn't sound exactly like a motorbike, but it was as close as I was going to get at 5 years old.

Think back to when you were younger and what you enjoyed doing.

What 5 things can you think of?

1. ....

2. ....

3. ....

4. ....

5. ....

If you can't afford certain things, then you can always find many things that you can enjoy.

When I was in my junior school, I was quite content playing a game of marbles.

Or I'd play 'pitch and toss' with my friends, which is where you play for pennies and throw a penny next to a wall to see who gets closest to the wall. If your coin is closest you win.

If you were a real 'high-roller' you would sometimes play with a two pence or even a 5 pence piece!

Having money can definitely take some challenges away, but it is not THE answer to total bliss, happiness, and fulfilment!

"It isn't what you have or who you are or where you are or what you were doing that makes you happy or unhappy. It is what you think about it.
Dale Carnegie

14 – EXERCISE

"If you are in a bad mood go for a walk. If you are still in a bad mood go for another walk."
Hippocrates

Happy

Hippocrates was an ancient Greek physician and was considered to be one of the most important figures in the history of medicine.

He is also referred to by some as the 'The Father of Medicine.'

Some have also credited Hippocrates with being the first person to believe people died of natural causes rather than superstition or the Gods.

Of course, you could still argue that it was God who put the disease into somebody's body, or it was God that sent the bus that knocked you down, but that argument is for someone else's book; and while that type of argument goes on about theories, I'd rather stick to certainties that can help you.

Anyhow, Hippocrates was rocking the scene from 460 BC to 370 BC.

He died at the grand old age of 90 years old.

Many people will live to 90 years old today, and actually, the average life expectancy, depending on which country you are born in, is closer to 80 years old in first world countries.

What was pretty outstanding about Hippocrates, was not only his vast knowledge as a physician; he also survived for so many years at a time when people usually kicked the bucket at a much younger age than they do today.

An article published in 'Scientific American' said that we are now living in an era where three generations coexist, which is called the evolution of grandparents.

Whereas, in some eras of human history, three generations would not have existed, and the grandparents would've died at a much younger age.

In other words, Hippocrates knew his stuff and was a big fan of exercise!

By now we should all know many of the benefits of exercise, so you may think there's no need for me to go on about them, but I will.

Not to teach you something you already know, but to

reinforce what you probably know anyways so that it can motivate you to do some form of exercise.

And the sooner you do it, the more benefits you will reap.

You may be reading this book at 11pm and might be thinking about going to bed.

But why not do 5 press-ups (or whatever number you can do) before bed?

Many people think doing five press-ups is insignificant and it will not make a difference.

They may also think that just going for a 400-metre walk is totally insignificant, but if it's 400-metres more than you did yesterday, or the day before, then it is significant!

Why?

Because you're making progress!

It's the same with the press-ups.

If you did 10 press-ups today, and you never did 10 press-ups yesterday, you're making progress!

So, the goal is to simply do a 'little bit more' than you've done before.

When it comes to happiness, it's more about taking action and getting into the habit of doing some form of physical exercise, than it is achieving some massive feat of human endurance.

There are so many people in this world today with mental challenges, heck let's face it, we all have mental challenges at one time or another!

Whether that challenge comes from the loss of a loved one or it comes from physical pain, which also has an effect on the mind.

But before we go reaching for pills from the doctor, the best thing to do is some form of exercise.

The renowned Harvard Medical School did a report several years ago on the benefits of exercise.

Some of the benefits are:

- Stress Reduction

- Anxiety Reduction

- Helps Fight Depression

The website www.womansday.com says, "exercise not only changes your body, it changes your mind, your attitude and your mood. Exercise should be regarded as a tribute to your heart. Good things come to those who sweat."

You probably don't need me to tell you this, but if you exercise on a regular basis and eat a balanced diet then, chances are, you're going to be a happier person overall.

At the end of the day, yeah it's all about taking action!

Reading words in a book is one thing but putting those words into action is where people who are struggling become winners in the game of life!

Apart from numerous studies that have been done on the benefits of exercise and how it helps happiness, from my own personal experience, I know that after I've exercised I always feel better for having done it.

I not only feel better for having done it, but in doing it my body is able to be in better working condition. As a result it's going to be more efficient with daily activities like walking up stairs or carrying things.

Exercise also keeps my body fat down and this gives me a psychological boost.

There is nothing wrong with being overweight if that is how you want to live your life.

Frankly, it's none of my business how you live your life, and there are many people out there that are confident, happy and big, which is all cool by me.

I'm just one of those people that enjoys the benefits and the results of exercise.

Love it or hate it, when it comes to having a better state of mind and better mental health, exercise makes the difference!

EPILOGUE

Happy

It's worth mentioning again, that finding happiness is, in one form or another, in all of my books.

This book serves as only a brief, but I hope, important guide to you finding more happiness and living a better life.

When all is said and done, no matter

- What country you live in.
- What race you belong to.
- What your beliefs are.
- Whether you're a man or a woman.

None of it ultimately matters!

What does matter is

"It's up to us as individuals to decide whether or not we are going to be happy!"

Too many people wait for happiness, too many people pursue happiness.

Happiness is a state of mind and to a great extent, you CAN control your thoughts!

DECIDE TO BE GRATEFUL FOR WHAT YOU HAVE AND BE HAPPY NOW!

LOVE,
MARK xx

Epilogue

ACKNOWLEDGEMENTS

It's almost impossible to say how many people have helped me along the way with producing this book, and if you're not in the acknowledgements just know that I am very grateful for your support and help.

However, I would like to say a massive THANK YOU to a few people that I can think of, off the top of my head:

Paul 'The Viking' Hughes, Tom Webb, Eva Savage, Mark 'Billy' Billingham, Julie Colombino-Billingham, Tracy, Kay and Maria Morris, Cheryl Hicks, Jamie Baulch, Gene Hipgrave, Tom Hughes, Kauri-Romet Aadamsoo, Mark Dawson, Craig Martelle, Michael Anderle, Michael and Emma Byrne, Paul 'Faz' Farrington, Paul Heaney, James Atkinson and Laura Taylor.

Also, a huge THANKS to 'The Mark Llewhellin Advance Reader Team' for taking the time to read the manuscript and make suggestions.

Live Your Dreams!

Mark

ABOUT THE AUTHOR

In 1990, Mark Llewhellin left school without knowing his grades. He had little confidence and was not at all optimistic about his future.

Not knowing what to do with his life Mark followed some of his friends into the Army. He failed his basic 1.5-mile run, was bullied, and was also voted the fattest person in the Troop!

After a year with the Junior Leaders Regiment Royal Artillery, Mark decided he would try and get into 29 Commando Regiment Royal Artillery, which is an elite Army Commando Regiment that at the time proudly held the Military Marathon World Record (i.e. a marathon carrying a 40lbs backpack).

After failing the 29 Commando Selection phase (called 'The Beat Up') twice, first through lack of fitness and secondly through an injury, Mark subsequently passed on his third attempt and completed the 'All Arms Commando Course' on his first attempt.

Mark later went on to achieve the following:

- Break the 100-kilometre Treadmill World Record.

- Place 1st in the Strava Distance Challenge in 2015 competing against over 51,000 runners.

- Place 1st in the Strava Distance Challenge in 2014 competing against over 40,000 runners.

- Run and walk 70-miles without training on his 40th birthday.

- Become a successful Personal Fitness Trainer.

- Complete the Marathon Des Sables (a six-day, 135-mile ultra-marathon in the Sahara Desert).

- Work and live in London's exclusive Park Lane as a Bodyguard.

- Run 1,620 miles in the United States whilst carrying a 35lbs pack.

Mark has interviewed some of the world's top performers and high achievers in various locations, including one of the world's most prestigious memorabilia rooms...the Hard Rock Café Vault Room in London.

He has travelled to over 50 countries and has been featured in leading national newspapers and on TV for his running achievements.

Mark has extensively worked in the support and care industry for many years helping individuals with brain injury, autism, epilepsy, dyspraxia, and various types of learning difficulties.

He is the Managing Director of Mark 7 Productions, as well as the Producer and Host of 'An Audience with Mark Billy Billingham' speaking events around the UK.

Mark is currently working on more personal development books and lives with his son Léon (when Léon's not at his Mum's) on a beautiful marina in South West Wales.

ALSO BY MARK LLEWHELLIN

THE UNDERDOG – Achieving Your Dreams Against the Odds

DELUSIONS OF GRANDEUR – How To Become More Than You Ever Dreamed Possible

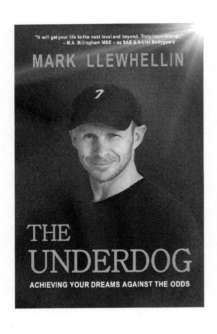

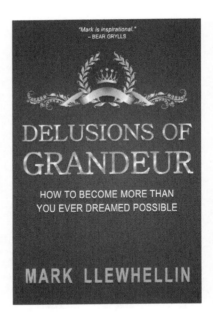

IF YOU ENJOYED THIS BOOK

Your help in spreading the word about Mark's books is greatly appreciated and your reviews make a huge difference to help new readers change their lives for the better.

If you found this book useful please leave a review on the platform you purchased it on.

MARK LLEWHELLIN BOOKS OUT IN 2020

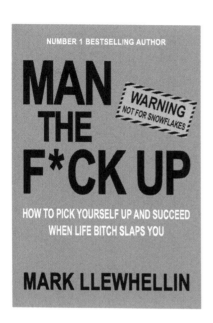

NUMBER 1 BESTSELLING AUTHOR

MAN
THE
F*CK UP

WARNING
NOT FOR SNOWFLAKES

HOW TO PICK YOURSELF UP AND SUCCEED
WHEN LIFE BITCH SLAPS YOU

MARK LLEWHELLIN

NUMBER 1 BESTSELLING AUTHOR

THE
SNOWFLAKE
SOCIETY

WARNING
NOT FOR BIG GIRLS BLOUSES

DEVELOP EXTREME MENTAL TOUGHNESS
WHILE LIVING IN THE WEAKEST
GENERATION IN HUMAN HISTORY

MARK LLEWHELLIN

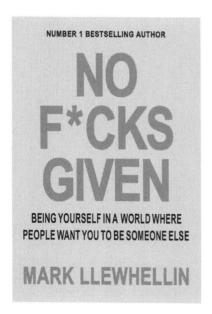

NUMBER 1 BESTSELLING AUTHOR

NO
F*CKS
GIVEN

BEING YOURSELF IN A WORLD WHERE
PEOPLE WANT YOU TO BE SOMEONE ELSE

MARK LLEWHELLIN

NUMBER 1 BESTSELLING AUTHOR

EXCEPTIONAL

BECOME THE BEST YOU CAN BE
ACHIEVE OUTSTANDING RESULTS

MARK LLEWHELLIN

GET TWO FREE MARK LLEWHELLIN BOOKS AND DEALS AND UPDATES

Join 'The Mark Llewhellin Advance Reader Team' for information on new books and deals plus:

You can pick up FREE copies of Mark's five star reviewed books:

1. 'The Underdog'

2. 'Delusions of Grandeur'

Simply go to Mark's website at www.markllewhellin.com and sign up for FREE.

DISCLAIMER

Although the author and publisher have made every effort to ensure that the information contained in this book was accurate at the time of release, the author and publisher do not assume and hereby disclaim any liability to any party for any loss, damage, or disruption caused by errors or omissions in this book, whether such errors or omissions result from negligence, accident, or any other cause.

A Mark 7 Publications Paperback.

First published in Great Britain in 2020

by Mark 7 Publications

ISBN 978-0-9956501-9-0

Book design and formatting by Tom Webb
pixelfiddler@hotmail.co.uk

Printed in Great Britain
by Amazon